# Table of Contents

# Original Ranch® Oyster Crackers

**1 box (16 ounces) oyster crackers**
**¼ cup vegetable oil**
**1 packet (1 ounce) HIDDEN VALLEY® The Original Ranch® Salad Dressing & Seasoning Mix**

Place crackers in a gallon-size Glad® Fresh Protection Bag. Pour oil over crackers. Seal bag and toss to coat. Add salad dressing & seasoning mix; toss again until coated. Spread evenly on large baking sheet. Bake at 250°F for 15 to 20 minutes.                    *Makes 8 cups*

# Original Ranch® Snack Mix

**8 cups KELLOGG'S® CRISPIX®* cereal**
**2½ cups small pretzels**
**2½ cups bite-size Cheddar cheese crackers (optional)**
**3 tablespoons vegetable oil**
**1 packet (1 ounce) HIDDEN VALLEY® The Original Ranch® Salad Dressing & Seasoning Mix**

*\*Kellogg's® and Crispix® are registered trademarks of Kellogg Company.*

Combine cereal, pretzels and crackers in a gallon-size Glad® Zipper Storage Bag. Pour oil over mixture. Seal bag and toss to coat. Add salad dressing & seasoning mix; seal bag and toss again until coated.          *Makes 10 cups*

Top to bottom: Original Ranch® Snack Mix
and Original Ranch® Oyster Crackers

# Hot Artichoke Dip

**1 envelope LIPTON® RECIPE SECRETS® Onion Soup Mix\***
**1 can (14 ounces) artichoke hearts, drained and chopped**
**1 cup HELLMANN'S® or BEST FOODS® Mayonnaise**
**1 container (8 ounces) sour cream**
**1 cup shredded Swiss or mozzarella cheese (about 4 ounces)**

*\*Also terrific with LIPTON® RECIPE SECRETS® Savory Herb with Garlic, Golden Onion, or Onion Mushroom Soup Mix.*

**1.** Preheat oven to 350°F. In 1-quart casserole, combine all ingredients.

**2.** Bake, uncovered, 30 minutes or until heated through.

**3.** Serve with your favorite dippers. *Makes 3 cups dip*

**Cold Artichoke Dip:** Omit Swiss cheese. Stir in, if desired, ¼ cup grated Parmesan cheese. Do not bake.

**Recipe Tip:** When serving hot dip for a party, try baking it in 2 smaller casseroles. When the first casserole is empty, replace it with the second one, fresh from the oven.

**Prep Time:** 5 minutes
**Bake Time:** 30 minutes

# Zesty Liver Pâté

**⅓ cup butter or margarine**
**1 pound chicken livers**
**¾ cup coarsely chopped green onions**
**¾ cup chopped fresh parsley**
**½ cup dry white wine**
**¾ teaspoon TABASCO® brand Pepper Sauce**
**½ teaspoon salt**
**Crackers or French bread**

Melt butter in large saucepan; add chicken livers, onions and parsley. Sauté until livers are evenly browned and cooked through. Transfer to blender or food processor container. Add wine, TABASCO® Sauce and salt; cover. Process until smooth. Pour into decorative crock-style jar with lid. Chill until thick enough to spread. Serve with crackers or French bread.

*Makes about 2 cups pâté*

Hot Artichoke Dip

# Spicy Shrimp Cocktail

- **2 tablespoons olive or vegetable oil**
- **¼ cup finely chopped onion**
- **1 tablespoon chopped green bell pepper**
- **1 clove garlic, minced**
- **1 can (8 ounces) CONTADINA® Tomato Sauce**
- **1 tablespoon chopped pitted green olives, drained**
- **¼ teaspoon red pepper flakes**
- **1 pound cooked shrimp, chilled**

1. Heat oil in small skillet. Add onion, bell pepper and garlic; sauté until vegetables are tender. Stir in tomato sauce, olives and red pepper flakes.

2. Bring to a boil; simmer, uncovered, for 5 minutes. Cover.

3. Chill thoroughly. Combine sauce with shrimp in small bowl.

*Makes 6 servings*

**Note:** Serve over mixed greens, if desired.

**Prep Time:** 6 minutes
**Cook Time:** 10 minutes

# Ortega® 7-Layer Dip

- **1 can (16 ounces) ORTEGA® Refried Beans**
- **1 package (1.25 ounces) ORTEGA Taco Seasoning Mix**
- **1 container (8 ounces) sour cream**
- **1 container (8 ounces) refrigerated guacamole**
- **1 cup (4 ounces) shredded cheddar cheese**
- **1 cup ORTEGA Salsa Homestyle Mild**
- **1 can (4 ounces) ORTEGA Diced Green Chiles**
- **2 large green onions, sliced**
  **Tortilla chips**

**COMBINE** beans and seasoning mix in small bowl. Spread bean mixture in 8-inch square baking dish.

**TOP** with sour cream, guacamole, cheese, salsa, chiles and green onions. Serve with chips.

*Makes 10 to 12 servings*

**Note:** Can be prepared up to 2 hours ahead and refrigerated.

Spicy Shrimp Cocktail

# Artichoke Frittata

**1 can (14 ounces) artichoke hearts, drained**
**3 teaspoons olive oil, divided**
**½ cup minced green onions**
**5 eggs**
**½ cup (2 ounces) shredded Swiss cheese**
**2 tablespoons grated Parmesan cheese**
**1 tablespoon minced fresh parsley**
**1 teaspoon salt**
**Black pepper**

**1.** Chop artichoke hearts; set aside.

**2.** Heat 2 teaspoons oil in 10-inch skillet over medium heat. Add green onions; cook and stir until tender. Remove from skillet.

**3.** Beat eggs in medium bowl until light. Stir in artichokes, green onions, cheeses, parsley, salt and pepper.

**4.** Heat remaining 1 teaspoon oil in same skillet over medium heat. Pour egg mixture into skillet. Cook 4 to 5 minutes or until bottom is lightly browned. Place large plate over skillet; invert frittata onto plate. Return frittata, uncooked side down, to skillet. Cook about 4 minutes more or until center is just set. Cut into small wedges. *Makes 12 to 16 appetizer servings*

# Lipton® Onion Dip

**1 envelope LIPTON® RECIPE SECRETS® Onion Soup Mix**
**1 container (16 ounces) sour cream**

**1.** In medium bowl, combine ingredients; chill, if desired.

**2.** Serve with your favorite dippers. *Makes 2 cups dip*

**Salsa Onion Dip:** Stir in ½ cup of your favorite salsa.

**Prep Time:** 5 minutes

Artichoke Frittata

# Gorgonzola Buffalo Wings

**DRESSING**

¼ **cup mayonnaise**
3 **tablespoons sour cream**
1½ **tablespoons white wine vinegar**
¼ **teaspoon sugar**
⅓ **cup (1½ ounces) BELGIOIOSO® Gorgonzola**

**CHICKEN**

2 **pounds chicken wings**
3 **tablespoons hot pepper sauce**
1 **tablespoon vegetable oil**
1 **clove garlic, minced**

**FOR DRESSING**

Combine mayonnaise, sour cream, vinegar and sugar in small bowl. Stir in BelGioioso Gorgonzola; cover and refrigerate until serving.

**FOR CHICKEN**

Place chicken in large resealable plastic food storage bag. Combine pepper sauce, oil and garlic in separate small bowl; pour over chicken. Seal bag tightly; turn to coat. Marinate in refrigerator at least 1 hour or, for hotter flavor, up to 24 hours, turning occasionally.

Prepare grill. Drain chicken, discarding marinade. Place chicken on grill. Grill on covered grill over medium-hot coals 25 to 30 minutes or until chicken is no longer pink, turning 3 to 4 times. Serve with dressing.    *Makes 4 servings*

# Sweet and Sour Meatballs

**MEATBALLS**

- ½ **cup instant rice**
- 2 **pounds 90% lean ground beef**
- 1 **egg**
- 1 **cup soft butter-flavored cracker crumbs***
- 2 **tablespoons CRISCO® Oil**

**SAUCE**

- 1½ **cups barbecue sauce**
- 1 **cup (12-ounce jar) SMUCKER'S® Pineapple Topping**
- ¼ **cup firmly packed brown sugar**

*You can substitute croutons or stuffing mix for the crackers.*

1. Prepare rice according to package directions.

2. Meanwhile, combine ground beef, egg and cracker crumbs; mix well. Add cooked rice; mix thoroughly. Shape into 1½- or 2-inch meatballs. Cook in oil over medium heat until browned, turning occasionally. If necessary, drain grease from skillet.

3. Combine all sauce ingredients; mix until brown sugar is dissolved. Pour over meatballs. Cover and simmer over low heat for 30 to 45 minutes or until meatballs are no longer pink in center. Serve with toothpicks.

*Makes 4 to 6 servings*

# The Ultimate Onion

 3 cups cornstarch
3½ cups all-purpose flour, divided
 6 teaspoons paprika, divided
 2 teaspoons garlic salt
1½ teaspoons black pepper, divided
 1 teaspoon salt
 2 bottles (12 ounces each) beer
 4 to 6 colossal onions (4 inches in diameter)
 2 teaspoons garlic powder
 ¾ teaspoon cayenne pepper, divided
 1 pint (2 cups) mayonnaise
 1 pint (2 cups) sour cream
 ½ cup chili sauce

**1.** For batter, mix cornstarch, 1½ cups flour, 2 teaspoons paprika, garlic salt, 1 teaspoon black pepper and salt in large bowl. Add beer; mix well. Set aside.

**2.** Cut about ¾ inch off top of each onion; peel onions. Being careful not to cut through bottom, cut each onion into 12 to 16 wedges.

**3.** Soak cut onions in ice water for 10 to 15 minutes. If onions do not "bloom," cut petals slightly deeper. Meanwhile, prepare seasoned flour mixture. Combine remaining 2 cups flour, remaining 4 teaspoons paprika, garlic powder, remaining ½ teaspoon black pepper and ¼ teaspoon cayenne pepper in large bowl; mix well.

**4.** Dip onions into seasoned flour mixture; remove excess by shaking gently. Dip in batter; gently shake to remove excess. Separate "petals" to coat thoroughly with batter. (If batter begins to separate, mix thoroughly before using.)

**5.** Gently place onions, one at a time, in fryer basket and deep-fry at 375°F 1½ minutes. Turn onion over and fry 1 to 1½ minutes or until golden brown. Drain on paper towels. Place onion upright in shallow bowl and remove about 1 inch of "petals" from center.

**6.** To prepare Creamy Chili Sauce, combine mayonnaise, sour cream, chili sauce and remaining ½ teaspoon cayenne pepper in large bowl; mix well. Serve with warm onions. *Makes about 24 servings*

*Favorite recipe from **National Onion Association***

The Ultimate Onion

# Festive Taco Cups

　1　tablespoon vegetable oil
　½　cup chopped onion
　½　pound ground turkey or ground beef
　1　clove garlic, minced
　½　teaspoon dried oregano leaves
　½　teaspoon chili powder or taco seasoning
　¼　teaspoon salt
1¼　cups shredded taco-flavored cheese or Mexican cheese
　　　blend, divided
　1　can (11½ ounces) refrigerated corn breadstick dough
　　　Chopped fresh tomato and sliced green onion for garnish
　　　(optional)

**1.** Heat oil in large skillet over medium heat. Add onion and cook until tender. Add turkey; cook until turkey is no longer pink, stirring occasionally. Stir in garlic, oregano, chili powder and salt. Remove from heat and stir in ½ cup cheese; set aside.

**2.** Preheat oven to 375°F. Lightly grease 36 miniature (1¾-inch) muffin pan cups. Remove dough from container but do not unroll dough. Separate dough into 8 pieces at perforations. Divide each piece into 3 pieces; roll or pat each piece into 3-inch circle. Press circles into prepared muffin pan cups.

**3.** Fill each cup with 1½ to 2 teaspoons turkey mixture. Bake 10 minutes. Sprinkle tops of taco cups with remaining ¾ cup cheese; bake 2 to 3 minutes more until cheese is melted. Garnish with tomato and green onion, if desired.

*Makes 36 taco cups*

CLASSIC APPETIZERS

Festive Taco Cups

# Cheese Straws

½ cup (1 stick) butter, softened
⅛ teaspoon salt
   Dash ground red pepper
1 pound sharp Cheddar cheese, shredded, at room
   temperature
2 cups self-rising flour

Heat oven to 350°F. In mixer bowl, beat butter, salt and pepper until creamy. Add cheese; mix well. Gradually add flour, mixing until dough begins to form a ball. Form dough into ball with hands. Fit cookie press with small star plate; fill with dough according to manufacturer's directions. Press dough onto cookie sheets in 3-inch-long strips (or desired shapes). Bake 12 minutes or just until lightly browned. Cool completely on wire rack. Store tightly covered.

*Makes about 10 dozen*

*Favorite recipe from **Southeast United Dairy Industry Association, Inc.***

# Potato Skins

4 baked potatoes, quartered
¼ cup sour cream
1 packet (1 ounce) HIDDEN VALLEY® The Original Ranch® Salad
   Dressing & Seasoning Mix
1 cup (4 ounces) shredded Cheddar cheese
   Sliced green onions and/or bacon pieces* (optional)

*Crisp-cooked, crumbled bacon can be used.*

Scoop potato out of skins; combine potatoes with sour cream and salad dressing & seasoning mix. Fill skins with mixture. Sprinkle with cheese. Bake at 375°F. for 12 to 15 minutes or until cheese is melted. Garnish with green onions and/or bacon pieces, if desired.

*Makes 8 to 10 servings*

Cheese Straws

# 7-Layer Ranch Dip

**1 envelope LIPTON® RECIPE SECRETS® Ranch Soup Mix**
**1 container (16 ounces) sour cream**
**1 cup shredded lettuce**
**1 medium tomato, chopped (about 1 cup)**
**1 can (2.25 ounces) sliced pitted ripe olives, drained**
**¼ cup chopped red onion**
**1 can (4.5 ounces) chopped green chilies, drained**
**1 cup shredded Cheddar cheese (about 4 ounces)**

**1.** In 2-quart shallow dish, combine soup mix and sour cream.

**2.** Evenly layer remaining ingredients, ending with cheese. Chill, if desired.
Serve with tortilla chips. *Makes 7 cups dip*

**Prep Time:** 15 minutes

# Awesome Antipasto

**1 jar (16 ounces) mild cherry peppers, drained**
**1 jar (9 ounces) artichoke hearts, drained**
**½ pound asparagus spears, cooked**
**½ cup pitted black olives**
**1 red onion, cut into thin wedges**
**1 green bell pepper, sliced into rings**
**1 red bell pepper, sliced into rings**
**1 bottle (8 ounces) Italian salad dressing**
**1 cup shredded Parmesan cheese, divided**
**1 package (6 ounces) HILLSHIRE FARM® Hard Salami**

Layer cherry peppers, artichoke hearts, asparagus, olives, onion and bell
peppers in 13×9-inch glass baking dish.

Pour dressing and ⅓ cup cheese over vegetables. Cover; refrigerate 1 to
2 hours.

Drain vegetables, reserving marinade. Arrange vegetables and Hard Salami in
rows on serving platter. Drizzle with reserved marinade. Top with remaining
⅔ cup cheese. *Makes 6 servings*

7-Layer Ranch Dip

# Honey-Mustard Chicken Wings

**3 pounds chicken wings**
**1 teaspoon salt**
**1 teaspoon black pepper**
**½ cup honey**
**½ cup barbecue sauce**
**2 tablespoons spicy brown mustard**
**1 clove garlic, minced**
**3 to 4 thin lemon slices**

## SLOW COOKER DIRECTIONS

**1.** Rinse chicken and pat dry. Cut off wing tips; discard. Cut each wing at joint to make two pieces. Sprinkle salt and pepper on both sides of chicken. Place wing pieces on broiler rack. Broil 4 to 5 inches from heat about 10 minutes, turning halfway through cooking time. Place broiled chicken wings in slow cooker.

**2.** Combine honey, barbecue sauce, mustard and garlic in small bowl; mix well. Pour sauce over chicken wings. Top with lemon slices. Cover; cook on LOW 4 to 5 hours.

**3.** Remove and discard lemon slices. Serve wings with sauce.

*Makes about 24 appetizers*

**Prep Time:** 20 minutes
**Cook Time:** 4 to 5 hours

Honey-Mustard Chicken Wings

# Easy Spinach Appetizer

2 **tablespoons butter**
3 **eggs**
1 **cup milk**
1 **cup all-purpose flour**
1 **teaspoon baking powder**
1 **teaspoon salt**
4 **cups (16 ounces) shredded Monterey Jack cheese**
2 **packages (10 ounces each) frozen chopped spinach, thawed and well drained**
½ **cup diced red bell pepper**

**1.** Preheat oven to 350°F. Melt butter in 13×9-inch pan.

**2.** Beat eggs in medium bowl. Add milk, flour, baking powder and salt; beat until well blended. Stir in cheese, spinach and bell pepper; mix well. Spread mixture over melted butter in pan.

**3.** Bake 40 to 45 minutes or until firm. Let stand 10 minutes before cutting into triangles or squares. *Makes 2 to 4 dozen pieces*

**Tip:** Easy Spinach Appetizer can also be made ahead, frozen and reheated. After baking, cool completely and cut into squares. Transfer squares to cookie sheet; place cookie sheet in freezer until squares are frozen solid. Transfer to resealable plastic food storage bag. To serve, reheat squares in 325°F oven for 15 minutes.

Easy Spinach Appetizer

# Thai Satay Chicken Skewers

**1** pound boneless skinless chicken breasts
**⅓** cup soy sauce
**2** tablespoons fresh lime juice
**2** cloves garlic, minced
**1** teaspoon grated fresh ginger
**¾** teaspoon red pepper flakes
**2** tablespoons water
**¾** cup canned unsweetened coconut milk
**1** tablespoon creamy peanut butter
**4** green onions with tops, cut into 1-inch pieces

**1.** Cut chicken crosswise into ⅜-inch-wide strips; place in shallow glass dish.

**2.** Combine soy sauce, lime juice, garlic, ginger and red pepper flakes in small bowl. Reserve 3 tablespoons mixture; cover and refrigerate. Add water to remaining mixture. Pour over chicken; toss to coat well. Cover; marinate in refrigerator at least 30 minutes or up to 2 hours, stirring mixture occasionally.

**3.** Soak 8 (10- to 12-inch) bamboo skewers 20 minutes in cold water to prevent them from burning; drain. Prepare grill for direct cooking.

**4.** Meanwhile, for peanut sauce, combine coconut milk, 3 tablespoons reserved soy sauce mixture and peanut butter in small saucepan. Bring to a boil over medium-high heat, stirring constantly. Reduce heat and simmer, uncovered, 2 to 4 minutes or until sauce thickens. Keep warm.

**5.** Drain chicken; reserve marinade. Weave 3 to 4 chicken strips accordion-style onto each skewer, alternating with green onion pieces. Brush chicken and onions with reserved marinade. Discard remaining marinade.

**6.** Place skewers on grid. Grill skewers on uncovered grill over medium-hot coals 6 to 8 minutes or until chicken is cooked through, turning halfway through grilling time. Serve with warm peanut sauce for dipping.

*Makes 4 servings*

Thai Satay Chicken Skewers

# Nutty Bacon Cheeseball

- **1 package (8 ounces) cream cheese, softened**
- **½ cup milk**
- **2 cups (8 ounces) shredded sharp Cheddar cheese**
- **2 cups (8 ounces) shredded Monterey Jack cheese**
- **¼ cup (1 ounce) crumbled blue cheese**
- **¼ cup finely minced green onions (white parts only)**
- **1 jar (2 ounces) diced pimiento, drained**
- **10 slices bacon, cooked, drained, finely crumbled and divided**
- **¾ cup finely chopped pecans, divided**
- **Salt and black pepper to taste**
- **¼ cup minced fresh parsley**
- **1 tablespoon poppy seeds**

**1.** Beat cream cheese and milk in large bowl at low speed of electric mixer until blended. Add cheeses. Beat at medium speed until well mixed. Add green onions, pimiento, half of bacon and half of pecans. Beat at medium speed until well mixed. Add salt and pepper to taste. Transfer half of mixture to large piece of plastic wrap. Shape into ball; wrap tightly. Repeat with remaining mixture. Refrigerate at least 2 hours or until chilled.

**2.** Combine remaining bacon and pecans with parsley and poppy seeds in pie plate or large dinner plate. Remove plastic wrap from each ball; roll each in bacon mixture until well coated. Wrap each ball tightly in plastic wrap and refrigerate until ready to serve, up to 24 hours. *Makes about 24 servings*

Nutty Bacon Cheeseball

# Acknowledgments

The publisher would like to thank the companies and organizations listed below for the use of their recipes and photographs in this publication.

BelGioioso® Cheese, Inc.

Del Monte Corporation

The Hidden Valley® Food Products Company

Hillshire Farm®

McIlhenny Company (TABASCO® brand Pepper Sauce)

National Onion Association

Ortega®, A Division of B&G Foods, Inc.

Smucker's® trademark of The J.M. Smucker Company

Southeast United Dairy Industry Association, Inc.

Unilever Foods North America